COASTERS OF THE MANCHESTER SHIP CANAL

by

Bernard McCall

INTRODUCTION

The history of the Manchester Ship Canal has often been written and it is not the purpose of this book to delve further into this history. We offer some basic facts both here and in the captions where we try to put the ships into a historical and geographical context, but our main aim is to look at some of the coastal vessels which have used the Canal over the last four decades and, hopefully, to try to re-assert the importance of the Canal as a commercial artery at a time when there is a demand to move from less environmentally-friendly modes of transport to those which conserve our increasingly scarce resources. There is no doubt that in terms of energy use and environmental impact, waterborne transport far outstrips any other mode. Hopefully, the potential for increased commercial use of the Manchester Ship Canal and other waterways will soon become evident to politicians, planners and all involved directly in the transport of goods.

The first sod was cut at Eastham on 11 November 1887. The line of the Canal was divided into sections each with its own superintendent. Several books are available, all with splendid illustrations, describing the construction of the Canal which proceeded very quickly. The Canal was opened in sections, and the directors of the Manchester Ship Canal Company made the first full passage along their Canal on 7 December 1893. The first commercial passage of the full length of the Canal was made on 1 January 1894 and Queen Victoria officially opened the Canal on 21 May of that year.

The fact that it was completed so quickly is but one of several remarkable facts about the Canal, not all of which can be recounted in the limited space available in this book. It must not be forgotten that the Canal also had its own railway system, the largest private railway in the British Isles, thus making it a "multimodal hub" many decades before that dreadful phrase had been thought of. The Canal

enjoyed its heyday in the late 1950s and the decades since then have seen the total demise of that railway system and the decline of the Canal which in the 1990s was thought to be almost terminal, and all at a time when the east/west road links in the area have experienced ever-increasing congestion.

Selection of photographs has been very difficult indeed. I have tried to cover as many berths as seemed reasonable and including different types of vessel seen in the last 40 years. Some captions for the photographs suggest good vantage points for photography. There can be no doubt that one of the best ways to obtain good photographs is to participate in one of the regular cruises offered by Mersey Ferries. It seems remarkable that only two decades ago such cruises were arranged only twice each year and had to be chartered. The demand dwindled to such an extent that there were plans to end the cruises. However, redevelopment of the terminal docks in Salford has, ironically, revived interest in the cruises and these now operate regularly throughout the summer months. Indeed such is the demand that it is sometimes necessary to use two cruise vessels on the same day.

Finally I must acknowledge the considerable help so willingly given during the preparation of the book. My debt of gratitude must go firstly to the photographers who have loaned their precious material and who are credited individually beneath their images. Thanks must also go to Gilbert Mayes who has assisted with proof reading and given the benefit of his encyclopaedic knowledge of shipping. Finally I must thank the staff of Amadeus Press for once again producing a fine finished product.

Bernard McCall, Portishead   April 2006

Published by Bernard McCall, 400 Nore Road, Portishead, Bristol, BS20 8EZ, England. Website : www.coastalshipping.co.uk
Telephone/fax : 01275 846178. E-mail : bernard@coastalshipping.co.uk
All distribution enquiries should be addressed to the publisher.

Printed by Amadeus Press, Ezra House, West 26 Business Park, Cleckheaton, West Yorkshire, BD19 4TQ
Telephone : 01274 863210; fax : 01274 863211; e-mail : info@amadeuspress.co.uk; website : www.amadeuspress.co.uk

ISBN : 1-902953-24-X

Front cover : Approaching the locks at Eastham where the Manchester Ship Canal joins the River Mersey, is the **Baltzborg** (DNK, 300grt/63). She was built at Frederikshavn by Ĺrskovs Staalskibsvĺrft as **Jens Rand**, becoming **Juto** in 1974 and **Baltzborg** earlier in 1977. Three years later, she came into British ownership as **St Anne of Alderney**, this being shortened to **St Anne** when she was sold in 1986 to owners in St Kitts. She is thought to be still trading as such in the Caribbean. The photograph shows her outward bound from Northwich to Finland on 16 September 1977.

(Neil Burns)

Back cover : There are many vantage points for observing ships on the Canal, two of the most popular being the high level bridges at Latchford and Warburton. Passing beneath the latter on 24 February 1979 is the **Esso Purfleet** (GBR, 2838grt/67) inward bound to Mode Wheel oil berth. The tanker was built by Furness Shipbuilding Co Ltd, at Haverton Hill on the River Tees. Sold out of the Esso fleet in 1983, she was renamed **Prima Jemima**, later becoming **Thita Pegasus** (1986), **Rainbow** and **Dubai Star** (1987), **El Miura** and **Sicily** (1991, and finally **Africa** (1993). She was eventually wrecked on the island of Milos.

(Bernard McCall)

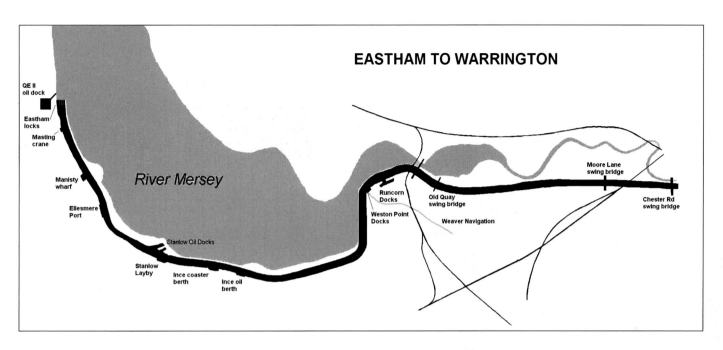

EASTHAM TO WARRINGTON

QE II oil dock

Eastham locks

Masting crane

River Mersey

Manisty wharf

Ellesmere Port

Stanlow Oil Docks

Stanlow Layby

Ince coaster berth

Ince oil berth

Runcorn Docks

Weston Point Docks

Old Quay swing bridge

Weaver Navigation

Moore Lane swing bridge

Chester Rd swing bridge

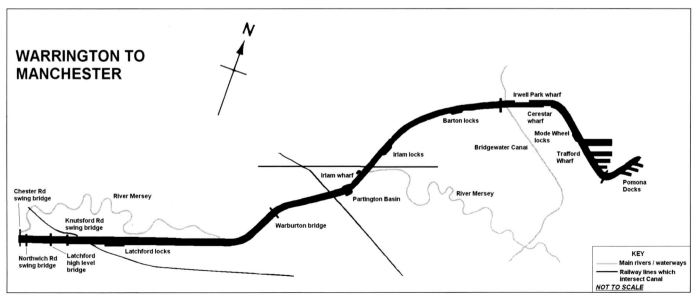

N

WARRINGTON TO MANCHESTER

Irwell Park wharf

Cerestar wharf

Barton locks

Mode Wheel locks

Bridgewater Canal

Trafford Wharf

Irlam locks

Pomona Docks

Irlam wharf

Partington Basin

River Mersey

Chester Rd swing bridge

River Mersey

Knutsford Rd swing bridge

Warburton bridge

Northwich Rd swing bridge

Latchford high level bridge

Latchford locks

KEY
Main rivers / waterways
Railway lines which intersect Canal
NOT TO SCALE

The Manchester Ship Canal joins the River Mersey at Eastham and this has always been a popular venue for day trippers. In days gone by, they would come by ferry from other points on the Mersey. The remains of the ferry pier have made an ideal vantage point for many years but recently they have been allowed to deteriorate and they are fenced off. There is also a Country Park at Eastham. Many ship photographers have found Eastham to be an ideal location with the sun over the shoulder and uncluttered background. However, moving back a few paces from the water's edge provides an alternative viewpoint which gives something of the atmosphere at Eastham. On 19 April 1980, the bitumen tanker **Robert M** (GBR, 1675gt/70) heads into the Mersey. Built by Hong Kong and Whampoa Dock Co Ltd and trading in the Caribbean as **Cree**, she was acquired by the Booker Group in 1977. Eventually coming into the ownership of the James Fisher group, she was sold in 1997 to operators in the Middle East who planned to trade her in the Persian Gulf as **Nesa I** but this name was changed to **Nesa R** before the end of 1997.

(Bernard McCall)

Emerging from the Queen Elizabeth II Oil Dock (see page 9) on 12 June 1982 is the *Svengulf Maersk* (DNK, 3918grt/65) which, along with sistership *Dangulf Maersk*, for many years delivered petroleum products from the Gulf Oil Company's refinery at Milford Haven usually to this dock. The tanker was built by Odense StaalskibsvÍrft. She was sold in 1982 being renamed *Petro Pyla*, later becoming *Scala* in 1996, *Iman* and *Iman II* in 1998. Our first two vessels have been tankers and such vessels have increasingly dominated the Canal's trade. Just visible on the shoreline ahead of the tanker is the viewing pier whilst the power station, now demolished, is in the far distance.

(Bernard McCall)

If the photograph on page 5 offered a rather unconventional view, we must also provide a "classic" view. On 8 March 2003, the **Knud Kosan** (IOM, 2252gt/82), ex **Knud Tholstrup**-91, **Traenafjord**-82, gets underway at the start of a voyage to Barry with styrene monomer. Built at the Nord-Offshore shipyard in Sandnessjoen, the tanker would have loaded her cargo at Runcorn Layby wharf. This view offers ample evidence of the reasons for the popularity of the location amongst photographers who prefer conventional uncluttered vantage points.

(Bernard McCall)

There are three lock chambers at Eastham, the smallest being originally intended for barges and now disused. The locks can be used for up to four hours on either side of high water and it has always been the custom to give priority to vessels leaving the Canal before high water. About to begin a voyage up the Canal and preparing to leave the smaller of the two locks now in use at Eastham on 26 March 1994 is the **Rosethorn** (GBR, 1213gt/82), ex **Shamrock Endeavour**-90. Just arriving in the larger lock is the **Greeba River** (IOM, 485gt/69). We shall see this vessel again but under a different name on page 34. By coincidence, both vessels were built at Hoogezand, the **Rosethorn** coming from the yard of Gebr. Coops whilst the **Greeba River** was built at the Bodewes yard. The large lock has dimensions of 600' x 80' (182,88m x 24,38m) and the smaller is 350' x 50' (106,68m x 15,24m).

(the late Mike Tomlinson)

With so many small rivers and water courses entering the Canal, all capable of swelling considerably during heavy rainfall, it was decided at the planning stage to have sluices at various points along the Canal in order to control water level. The water channel leading to the sluice gates at Eastham can be seen to the left of this view; this channel has always been a popular place for berthing tugs whilst they await their next turn of duty. Arriving in the large lock is the **Whitkirk** (GBR, 730gt/69), one of a group of tankers built for Bowker & King in the late 1960s and early 1970s to the maximum dimensions of the canal which links Sharpness to Gloucester. Originally named **Borman**, after twenty years delivering oil products in the Bristol Channel, she was purchased by Hull-based John H Whitaker (Tankers) Ltd and has worked in various parts of the UK. On the Mersey she has been used mainly as a bunkering vessel, sometimes delivering fuel to ferries in Holyhead. The photograph was taken on 31 August 2003. In 2005, she was retired from service and laid up in Birkenhead.

(Bernard McCall)

In the late 1940s, it became clear that the size of tankers used for the carriage of crude oil was set to increase and a decision was made to build a dock large enough to accommodate what was seen as a new generation of "supertankers". This dock, opened in January 1954, was located west of the main locks at Eastham and had its own entrance lock with dimensions of 807' x 100' (246 metres x 30,5 metres). On 15 January 2003, the *South Trader* (LIB, 3705gt/74), ex *Malik Trader*-97, *Plata*-96, *Bow Plata*-94, *Bow Cecil*-85, arrives in the Queen Elizabeth II lock. The tanker was built by Soviknes Verft in Sovik.

(C J Tabarin)

The photographs in this book now take us on an eastwards passage along the Canal. On the western bank of the Canal near Eastham are three berths, one of which was a designated layby berth used by vessels awaiting their turn in the locks or passage along the Canal. Adjacent to that is an oil berth known as the Sheerlegs oil berth and it is here that the **Sunny Fellow** (SGP, 1244grt/68), ex *Libra*-73, was photographed on 5 May 1980. This tanker was built at the Jos L Meyer yard in Papenburg, now more associated with the construction of large passenger ships. Sold in 1981, the tanker was renamed **Happy Bird** and in 1990 was sold yet again, now becoming **Australgas** and working in Chile. She disappeared from movement reports in early 1997 without news of change of name so she may have been scrapped at that time.

(Cedric Catt)

Outward bound from Weston Point and approaching Eastham on 9 August 1977 is the **La Paloma** (PAN, 499grt/61). A typical Dutch-built coaster of the early 1960s, she is a product of the Bodewes shipyard in Hoogezand and for the first ten years of her life she was named **Wedlooper**, becoming **Efficacia** in 1971, **Sus 1** in 1976 and **La Paloma** in 1977. She traded for four years under this name.

Her later history saw her renamed **Ken Ashby** in 1981, **Rhino S** in 1984, **Rhine** in 1985, **CTS Trader** in 1996 and then **Alba Marina** in 1999. She is still listed as such in *Lloyd's Register* with unidentified owners in Venezuela.

(Neil Burns)

11

Ocean-going vessels trading to and from the upper reaches of the Canal could sometimes find it necessary to have the top sections of masts and funnels removed in order to allow them to pass beneath bridges. At Eastham was a lay-by berth on which was located the 30-tonne masting crane used to remove and replace overheight equipment. This crane has now been demolished. One of its legs is just visible in this view of the **Briarthorn** (GBR, 1576gt/80) passing on 1 January 2001. This vessel was built as **Craigallian** by Richards (Shipbuilders) Ltd at Lowestoft, and took the name **Briarthorn** in 1989. In 2002, she was sold out of British ownership and hoisted the Panamanian flag as **O. K. Apostolos**. She was sold again in August 2004, now becoming **Moon** under the Netherlands Antilles flag.

(David Williams)

The **Joan T** (IRL, 397grt/58) was built by Gebr Barkmeijer in Veirverlaten. Originally named **Scheldt**, she traded for Dutch owners until sold in 1970 to Metcalf Motor Coasters Ltd, of London. Three years later she was bought by Michael G Tyrrell, of Arklow, and renamed **Joan T**. As such she was a regular visitor to the Canal. She was sold to other owners in 1985 and renamed **Elfi**. On 2 March 1987, her cargo shifted when she was on passage from Beckingham to Bremen and she had to be abandoned by her crew; she later capsized and sank.

She is seen here on 5 May 1980 inward bound from Arklow to Runcorn where she loaded salt for Belfast. The photograph was taken from the **Lady Mary** (PAN, 399grt/57) which was making the short voyage from Anderton to Liverpool. The masting crane can be seen in the middle distance whilst in the far distance is the power station, now demolished.

(Cedric Catt)

Probably the most difficult wharf for photography anywhere on the Canal is Manisty Wharf located on the south bank between Eastham and Ellesmere Port. Opposite the wharf on the northern bank is Mount Manisty, an artificial mound made from spoil dug from the Canal and without any means of public access. Consequently, photographs must be taken from vessels as they pass the wharf. Even this poses problems because not only will the photographer be shooting into whatever sun there may be but also the high embankment at this point means that the wharf itself is in shadow. It was on 12 June 1982 that the **Nielse Danielsen** (DNK, 1129grt/77) was photographed during a Canal cruise. On the quayside in the background can be seen a large quantity of logs, once a significant import at the berth which at one point in the 1980s was owned by the James Fisher group. The ship was built at the Bevr van Diepen yard in Waterhuizen as **Amigo Defender** and was renamed **Nielse Danielsen** in 1978. After trading thus for six years, she was sold and renamed **Atlantic Breeze** and a further sale in 1988 saw her become **Reifens**.

(Bernard McCall)

As noted in the previous caption, opposite Manisty Wharf lies Mount Manisty, made from excavated material. During construction, the Canal was divided into sections which were self-sufficient in men and equipment and had their own resident engineers and superintendents. Mount Manisty is named after the contractor's agent of the Eastham - Ellesmere Port section. Mr Manisty and his wife showed great concern for the labour force and did their best to ensure good working and social conditions for the workforce. Manisty Wharf itself has seen varied use over the years, perhaps being best known for the import of pulp and forest products for Bowaters paper mill. Exports have included newsprint from a paper mill at Shotton destined for Miami and, from a steel works at Shotton, steel used to be exported to the Great Lakes. In 2004, with an increasing demand for coal to fuel power stations, it was decided to use the wharf to import coal transhipped at the deepwater terminal at Hunterston on the Firth of Clyde. The coal is then taken to nearby Fiddlers Ferry power station. To service this trade, the **Clydenes** (NOR, 4783gt/95), formerly **Arklow Bridge**, built by Appledore Shipbuilders Ltd, was acquired from Arklow Shipping and chartered by Clydeport Ltd. She was photographed as she discharged her cargo of coal on 12 January 2006.

(Rosalind Thomas)

With Mount Manisty in the background, the **Anke Ehler** (DEU, 2606gt/90) is seen loading containers for Belfast at Ellesmere Port on 21 April 1992. The history of this town is fascinating, much of it built around canals notably the Shropshire Union Canal which were used to bring goods from the Midlands, Staffordshire and Cheshire to the Mersey for export. The coaster is berthed at the container terminal which had been used for services to the Iberian peninsula and Mediterranean but by 1992 was used almost exclusively for a service across the Irish Sea carrying coal in containers. The ship was built by J J Sietas and is an example of the yard's Type 130 multi-purpose standard design. In 1998, she was renamed **Apus** and became **Atlantic Coast** in 2003. Just visible in the distance is the **Siarkopol** (POL, 6964gt/74) inward bound from Gdansk with a cargo of liquid sulphur.

(Bernard McCall)

Many of the former warehouses in the old part of Ellesmere Port have been converted to form the Ellesmere Port Boat Museum which preserves much of the area's industrial and maritime archaeology. There has also been residential development on the Canal bank. This area is an ideal vantage point for ships sailing along the Canal. This book would be incomplete without a photograph of a Shell tanker, such vessels having been a familiar sight on the Canal for almost eighty years. Until the late 1970s, Shell tankers of up to 20,000 dwt called regularly, often bringing cargoes from the Caribbean. After their demise, the Shell presence was maintained by coastal tankers distributing products to the Channel Islands, Isle of Man, Ireland, and Scotland. On 11 May 1997, the **Asprella** (GBR, 1926gt/81) passes Ellesmere Port and approaches Stanlow. Built by the Goole Shipbuilding and Repairing Co Ltd as **Shell Seafarer**, she was given her traditional Shell name at a special ceremony in Ellesmere Port on 9 June 1993. In the late 1990s, Shell disposed of its own coastal fleet to F T Everard Shipping Ltd, and this vessel was renamed **Arduity**. Changing patterns of distribution have since meant that the tankers loaded in Milford Haven rather than the Ship Canal, causing a big reduction in the number of vessels using the Canal.

(Bernard McCall)

In recent years, trade on the upper reaches of the Canal has been dominated by the import of grain and more will be said about this later in the book. KD Marine currently operates two vessels on the Canal carrying grain from Liverpool to Manchester. In the autumn of 2005, a third vessel was acquired and, although intended for trade in Scotland, she has been used on the Canal. On page 42, we shall refer in greater detail to the original trade of the *Calemax Enterprise* (CKI, 507gt/74), ex *Elf*-05, *Sibir*-99, *Seacombe Trader*-98, built by the Yorkshire Drydock Co Ltd in Hull. She is seen passing Ellesmere Port in January 2006.

(Rosalind Thomas)

The Manchester Ship Canal Company began the construction of an oil dock on the estuary side of the Canal at Stanlow in 1916 and this was completed six years later. It was in 1923 that the company then known as Shell-Mex began to build a tank storage farm in the area. The handling of petroleum products grew so quickly that work soon started on a second, larger dock adjacent to the first and this was opened in 1933. The two docks served the Shell oil refinery but, as already noted, changes in distribution patterns in the last decade have resulted in a reduction in the use of these docks. On 10 August 2002, the **Pyla** (LUX, 4357gt/01) was noted in the oil dock. Launched as **Chemical Urkmez**, this tanker was built at Tuzla in Turkey by Celiktekne Sanayii ve Ticaret.

(Roy Cressey)

On the landward side of the Canal, there are seven berths within a two-mile stretch beginning with the Associated Octel berth to the west and ending with Ince power station berth to the east. It was at the Associated Octel berth that the **Orion Star** (ITA, 2691gt/84), ex **Orion Gas**-00, was photographed on 26 July 2001. A typical Japanese-built gas tanker, she was constructed by Kitanihon Zosen K. K. at Hachinohe.

(Bernard McCall)

The date of the previous photograph, 26 July 2001, proved to be a busy one at these berths. A larger tanker was at Stanlow Layby berth whilst two Stolt tankers occupied two of the berths at Ince. At Ince Oil Berth is the **Stolt Guillemot** (CYM, 3204gt/93), ex **Sasi Terkol**-96. She had sailed up the Canal to Partington two days previously.

(Dominic McCall)

At Ince Coaster Berth is sister vessel **Stolt Kite** (CYM, 3206gt/92), ex **Randi Terkol**-96. The sister vessels on this page were built at the Ãrhus Flydedok shipyard in Denmark and were part of a nine-ship order placed at this yard in 1990/91, the final one being the **Sasi Terkol**. In the mid-1990s, owners Terkol suffered severe cash flow problems and the company collapsed in summer 1996. Stolt-Nielsen bought some of the tankers and was able to integrate them seamlessly into its fleet as it already had others in the series on bareboat charter.

(Bernard McCall)

The **Atria** (DEU, 2673gt/86) would normally have called at the container terminal at Ellesmere Port but here she is heading up the Canal to load at Runcorn Salt Works. Of particular interest are the earthworks just visible to the port side of the coaster. These are part of Weston Mersey Locks, one of three sets of locks which provided a link between the Mersey and other canals and navigable rivers during the construction of the Manchester Ship Canal. These connections had to be maintained until the Canal was completed. The ship was built by J J Sietas and is a near-sistership of the **Anke Ehler** on page 16 but is two metres shorter. Sold in 1999, she was renamed **Emsbroker**, becoming **Kea** on 2 August 2000 and then **Arosita** only a few weeks later on 26 September. Sold to Swedish owners in 2002, she reverted to her original name.

(Danny Kelliher)

Before moving further along the Manchester Ship Canal, we shall look briefly at coasters on the Weaver Navigation which joins the Ship Canal at Marsh Lock on the outskirts of Weston Point. The landscape here is dominated by huge ICI factories which process and manufacture an immense number of chemicals. For many years, exports were taken from ICI's Castner Kellner works to the Du Pont factory at Maydown near Londonderry. A regular caller in this trade was the *Marwit* (NLD, 499grt/60), built by de Groot & van Vliet at Slikkerveer. Despite having the appearance of a general cargo vessel, she was classed as a "chemical carrier" and was equipped with cylindrical tanks in her hold for the carriage of chlorine. Sold in 1981, she was renamed *Sapna* but her new career seems to have been short-lived. She arrived at Chittagong on 11 February 1982, was arrested on 29 June 1983, and was aground two years later. This photograph was taken on 22 March 1976.

(Neil Burns)

The purpose-built **Northern Star** (1114gt/80) replaced the **Marwit** in the transportation of chlorine from Weston Point to Londonderry but, after a period laid up in Manchester following almost twenty years in service, she was sold in the summer of 2000 to Norwegian owners by whom she was renamed **Norvarg**. Her new owners provide bunkering and supply services to the Arctic fishing fleet. In her distinctive yellow livery, the **Northern Star** was photographed at Weston Point on 30 March 1996. She was built by Moss Rosenberg Verft in Norway.

(Richard McCart)

In late 1996 and early 1997, a new power station was built for ICI at Rock Savage on the outskirts of Runcorn. Several items of heavy equipment were delivered to a wharf some three miles from Marsh Lock. On 12 March 1997, the **Myrås** (NOR, 1208gt/85) brought a large piece of equipment from Gdynia. In the background can be seen the bridge carrying the M56 motorway over the Weaver Navigation.

The ship is one of three sisterships built at the Krögerwerft shipyard in Schacht-Audorf near Rendsburg. Handed over to her original German owners on 27 June 1985, she was named **Alko** and took her present name following sale to Norwegian owners in 1996.

(John Slavin)

The **Sheila Maria** (GBR, 397grt/57) is seen on the Weaver Navigation on a wintry 30 December 1979. She was heading for the swinging basin prior to berthing at Wallerscote, seen in the background, where she would load a cargo of soda ash for delivery to Dublin. Built by the C Amels & Zoon yard at Makkum, she typifies Dutch coaster building in the late 1950s. Built for the Wagenborg company as **Spaarneborg**, she was sold out of the fleet in 1972 to become **La Paloma**. Sold again in 1975, she was renamed **Cantium** and finally **Sheila Maria** in 1979. For the next five years, ownership and management seem to have changed frequently. In 1984, her then owners planned to trade her in west Africa and she left Ridham Dock on 24 February 1985 bound for Apapa/Lagos. Oddly, she found a return cargo from Douala for Selby but suffered engine problems and had to put into Dakar as port of refuge on 3 June 1985. With mounting financial problems, her British owners sold her to a local operator in Dakar in early 1986 - and nothing more has been heard of her.

(Neil Burns)

The vast ICI works on the outskirts of Northwich continues to produce and export vast quantities of soda ash. Rather than load this on to ships at the nearby wharf, the soda ash is taken by lorry to Garston where it is then loaded on to ships. There was no such nonsense on 19 April 1980 when the **Stevnsklint** (DNK, 451gt/63), a frequent caller, was waiting to load. Built by Husumer Schiffswerft, she was sold to other Danish owners in 1981 and renamed **Uno**, and a further sale ten years later saw her renamed **Thurø**. She still trades as such but now is owned by Spanish operators in Tenerife.

(Bernard McCall)

The last commercial vessel to use the Weaver Navigation on a regular basis was the purpose-built **Saint Kearan** (GBR, 439gt/78) which loaded calcium chloride liquor at Winnington on the outskirts of Northwich. With British Waterways unwilling to invest in dredging and infrastructure maintenance, the **Saint Kearan** was eventually unable to load full cargoes and she had to be topped off with cargo taken by road to a loading berth at Weston Church Wall on the Manchester Ship Canal. Sold to Norwegian owners in March 2001, she was renamed **Eide Tank 1** but later in that year was sold on to owners in Gibraltar and renamed **Georgie**. In the background of this photograph taken on 28 December 1996 can be seen the Anderton Lift, built to transport boats between the Weaver Navigation at the lower level and the Trent & Mersey Canal at the upper level.

(Bernard McCall)

Lying adjacent to the magnificent structure of the Anderton Lift is the small wharf at Anderton, now sadly disused. On 29 April 1980, however, it was very busy. The *Ida Maria* (DNK, 300grt/61) was waiting to waiting to discharge a cargo from Rochefort, probably talc. A product of the Nordsøværftet yard in Ringkøbing, she began life as *Elselil* and became *Laurentius* between 1974 and 1979 when she took the name *Ida Maria*. In September 1987, she was sold to Caribbean operators and renamed *Laurent*. The *Anna V* (CYP, 424grt/55) which had arrived from

Livorno was built by H Rancke in Hamburg as *Gunther*. She was lengthened in 1962 and renamed in 1973. Her later history is unknown. Completing the scene is the *Margreet* (NLD, 397gt/61) which sailed to Pasajes with scrap the following day. Built at the "Friesland" shipyard in Lemmer as *Schieborg*, she was renamed *Bonny* in 1972 and bore the name *Margreet* between 1976 and 1983 when she was renamed *Mrs White*. She later became *Ellenaki* (1987), *Helena Sea* (1989) and *Melinda D* (1997).

(Neil Burns)

Cargoes on the Weaver Navigation were always dominated by the ICI chemical industry but in the mid-1980s a successful marketing campaign saw a wide variety of import cargoes which included talc from France, magnesite from Spain and Greece, fertilisers from France and Germany, and fishmeal from Scotland. There were also imports of refractory materials from Iceland destined for use mainly in the Potteries. Exports included cement and building materials to Ireland and the Isle of Man. This would probably have been the destination of the ***Ben Varrey*** (IOM, 451grt/63) observed on 4 March 1979. Built by E J Smit & Zoon at Westerbroek, she spent her whole career working for the Ramsey Steamship Co Ltd, a career that was cut short when she suffered major engine problems in December 1984. She was eventually sold for scrap and was demolished at Millom in late 1985.

(Neil Burns)

Of huge commercial importance on the Weaver Navigation, Manchester Ship Canal and River Mersey were the series of vessels built over the years for ICI and its predecessors. These vessels carried chemicals often for transhipment and were a regular sight along the three waterways until the 1970s. Sporting the final vivid ICI livery of black and orange when photographed at the ICI works near Anderton on 18 April 1980 was the **James Jackson Grundy**, built locally at Northwich by W J Yarwood & Sons. Originally she had a tall foremast and derrick but these were removed long before the date of this photograph. Like several of her sisterships, she was eventually sold for further non-commercial use. Bought by the Northwich Sea Cadets for £1, she was renamed **TS Witch** and moored at the site of the former Yarwood yard. Later sold, after a period of neglect, she has been restored and reverted to her original name.

(Bernard McCall)

As we return to the Manchester Ship Canal, we take a brief look at Weston Point docks which for many years were owned by British Waterways. They were sold in 1989 and various operators have tried to revive them but without long-term success. In recent years, they have fallen into decline and have seen little use although vessels do call very occasionally with large items of equipment destined for the local ICI factories. On 3 October 1975, the **Emmy S** (NLD, 500grt/57), built at the Bijholt shipyard in Foxhol, lies in Weston Point. The following year, she was sold on to other Dutch owners and renamed **First** and in 1980 was bought by owners in the Middle East who renamed her **Inayet Allah**. There then followed a series of name changes which saw her become **Abdellatif** in 1981, **Faten** in 1986, **Abdellatif** (again) in 1990 and **Faten** (again) in 1991. In 1999, *Lloyd's Register* suggested that her entry should be deleted as her continued existence was in doubt.

(Neil Burns)

Noted at Weston Point on 11 May 1993 was the recently-renamed *Sea Boyne* (IRL, 1917gt/77). Built in Japan by Watanabe Zosen K. K. at Hakata, she was handed over to her German owners on 19 July 1977. Short charters saw her renamed *Scot Venture* in 1988 and *Echo Carrier* in 1989 before she reverted to *Sybille* in 1989. In 1991, she was sold to UK owners and, bareboat chartered into the expanding fleet of Dundalk Shipowners, was renamed *Rockabill*. After arrival at Goole on 28 March 1993, she was renamed *Sea Boyne*. There is still evidence of her former name in this view taken some six weeks later. Six years later, the vessel was sold to British owners and renamed *Sea Osprey*.

(Danny Kelliher)

Located some ten miles (sixteen kilometres) from Eastham is Runcorn Salt Works. The huge beds of rock salt beneath this area of north Cheshire have been worked since Roman times and they formed the basis for the chemical industry which now dominates the area. Salt is exported from a canalside wharf 600 feet (183 metres) long. The *Castor* (FIN, 2654grt/62) seems to be fully loaded and awaiting departure, almost certainly bound for Finland which was a regular destination for salt cargoes in the 1970s and 1980s. The ship was built at the Wärtsilä-Crichton shipyard in Turku, and was lengthened in 1968. Renamed *Stratus* after a sale within Finland in 1982, she left Finnish ownership in 1985 when she became *Olaf* under the Red Ensign. She sank off Den Helder on 7 July 1986 when on passage from Aalborg and although raised on 12 August, she was eventually scrapped in The Netherlands.

(Danny Kelliher)

There is no access to the canal bank opposite Runcorn Salt Works so the only effective way to obtain photographs is from a passing vessel. Such was the method used to obtain this view of the *Tora* (IOM, 398grt/69) in September 1986. This coaster was a regular visitor to the Ship Canal for many years and we have already seen her on page 7. She was built at the Bodewes yard in Hoogezand for the well-known Dutch owner Beck's as *Apollo 1* and was acquired by Arklow Shipping in November 1979, being renamed *Arklow River* in January 1980. In

1982, she moved to UK owners who renamed her *Cynthia June* and in 1986 she took the name *Tora* following purchase by Dublin owners but with management in the Isle of Man. Sold to Mezeron Ltd, also of the Isle of Man, in 1988 she was renamed *Greeba River*. She left northern Europe in 1997 following purchase by an owner in Newfoundland, Canada, for whom she trades as *Placentia Sound*.

(Ken Lowe)

34

Runcorn Docks are located 12 miles (19 kilometres) from Eastham and are now the only working dry cargo docks on the Canal. Historically, the docks are of great interest because they pre-date the construction of the Canal. Opposite the docks is the disused Bridgewater Lock, which once gave access to the Bridgewater Canal from the Mersey. The Ship Canal Company took over Runcorn Docks when it acquired the Bridgewater Canal, and it is worth noting that the docks continued to be operated by a separate department, the Bridgewater Department, within the Canal Company. Ironically, trade grew in the 1970s when the newly-constructed motorways in the area offered ready access to the docks. This growth was partly at the expense of the terminal docks at the eastern end of the Canal. This view at Runcorn was taken on 20 April 1976. The *Ivan Bolotnikov* (RUS, 1426gt/69) is member of a class of nineteen similar vessels built for the state-owned merchant fleet of the former Soviet Union by the Angyalfold Shipyard in Budapest. In 1997 she was sold and renamed *Svetlana*, becoming **Manta 1** in 1998 and **Eternal Love** in 2000. She was last heard of at Demerara in mid-2001. Also visible in this view are the **Tasmanie** (NLD, 490grt/56) and J & A Gardner's **Saint Enoch** (GBR, 785grt/59).

(Neil Burns)

Regular visitors to the Ship Canal were coasters from the S William Coe fleet. A fine example seen at Runcorn on 28 March 1976 is the **Firethorn** (GBR, 1062gt/67). She had arrived at Runcorn with a cargo of stone from Llanddulas and was waiting to load coal slack for delivery to Antwerp. Built at the J Pattje shipyard in Waterhuizen, she was sold out of the Coe fleet in 1991 and was renamed **Firestorm**, later becoming **Angelus** in 1992 and **Limerick** in 1994. As such she remains listed in the 2005/6 edition of *Lloyd's Register*, but without details of flag or ownership.

(Neil Burns)

In 1999/2000, there were great hopes that a new wharf, dedicated to the export of cement, at Weaste on the outskirts of Manchester would generate a considerable quantity of traffic. Sadly these hope have not been fulfilled. The wharf was rail-served and thus environmentally friendly. On 19 July 2000, the **Cem River** (VCT, 2962gt/72) passes Runcorn after loading the first cargo from the new wharf - some 3900 tonnes of cement destined for the Azores. After arrival in the Canal five days previously, she had been fitted with a collapsible mainmast to allow her to meet the Canal's air draught limitations. She was built at the J J Sietas shipyard, the first of this yard's two Type 74 vessels, and was completed as **Milburn Carrier** for New Zealand owners. She returned to northern Europe in 1989 after purchase by Arklow Shipping in whose fleet she spent seven years as **Arklow River**. In 1996, she was sold to Norwegian owners who named her **Cem River**. In early 2004, she was detained for a month at Newport because of many deficiencies and eventually sailed to Poland for permanent repairs. At about this time, she was renamed **Cem Rio** but seems not to have traded as such for by June she had returned to service named **Rhodos Cement**.

(Neil Burns)

There are two bridges over the Canal linking Runcorn to Widnes. The railway bridge was built between 1866 and 1868, thus predating the Canal. The designers had the good sense to realise that it should be built high enough to allow large vessels to pass beneath. A height of 75 feet (22,86m) was requested but in fact it was built at a height of 79' 7" (24,25m) above water level. The road crossing was a different matter. In 1905 a transporter bridge was constructed. This was a travelling platform suspended by cables from a high level girder span. By the 1950s, this bridge was no longer able to cope with all the traffic and it was replaced in 1961 by a new fixed bridge whose graceful arch is evident in this view. The Canal is at its narrowest at this point and the approach from the west includes the sharpest bend on the Canal. Rounding this bend on 23 July 1990 is the **Northgate** (IOM, 2071gt/81), one of four similar tankers built in Japan by Kanrei Zosen K.K. at Naruto for the Hull Gates Shipping Co Ltd. Ownership later passed through Rowbotham Tankships, P&O Tankships and the James Fisher group before she was sold in 2003 and renamed **East Wind**.

(Bernard McCall)

Having just seen the first fixed bridges on our eastbound journey along the Canal, we now find our first swing bridge only one mile further on. This is Old Quay swing bridge, visible to the left of this view, and is the first of seven similar swing bridges which take major roads across the Canal. The vessel, **Geminus** (NLD, 402gt/71), has an interesting history. She was built at the West Vlaamse shipyard in Oostkamp as **Dolfijn**. She was what was known as a "Denmark Trader", a vessel used to trade between Dutch and Danish ports, and is the last surviving example of this type. Such a route enabled these vessels to remain close to shore at all times. Because of the nature of this trade, she has two deadweight figures. With a deadweight of 530 dwt, she was allowed to navigate up to 50 nautical miles offshore; but when carrying cargo on inland waters, she had a permitted deadweight of 730dwt. Later name changes saw her become **Veritas** in 1975, **Bornrif** in 1979, **Zuiderzee** in 1983, and **Geminus** in 1985. In mid-2003, she was bought by Captain Heather Chaplin for trading in the north-west of England and has been employed in carrying grain cargoes from Liverpool to Manchester. She was photographed heading west on 4 December 2004. The proximity of the Canal to the Mersey at this point is very evident. On the opposite bank of the Mersey is the town of Widnes.

(Rosalind Thomas)

The second swing bridge to be passed on a voyage up the Canal is Moore Lane bridge. On 28 July 1980, the gas tanker **Sunny Baby** (NOR, 1363grt/65) approaches the bridge as she heads for Partington. She was built at Ulsteinvik by Kleven Mek Verksted as a dry cargo vessel named **Kings Star**. Sold in 1970, she was converted to a gas tanker and named **Sunny Baby**. Eleven years later, she was sold again and was renamed **Happy Falcon**, becoming **Kilgas Discovery** in 1992 and then **Mereb Gas** under the flag of Eritrea in 1999.

(Bernard McCall)

Between Moore Lane swing bridge and Chester Road swing bridge is Acton Grange wharf, now disused but once a busy container terminal with a regular service to Londonderry for DuPont chemicals. The **Klaus Block** (DEU, 500grt/69), photographed from the effluent tanker **Gibert J. Fowler** in September 1973, served the route for several years. Built by J J Sietas, she is one of only two examples of that yard's Type 64 design. She was sold in 1983 and was renamed **Gerd**, later becoming **Heimvik** in 1986 and **Nordgard** in 1989. Owned in Sweden until autumn 2005, she was then bought by Mediterranean operators who transferred her to the flag of North Korea but kept the name **Nordgard**.

(Ken Lowe)

There are three busy swing bridges passed in quick succession in Warrington, these being Chester Road bridge, Northwich Road bridge and Knutsford Road bridge. Passing the latter on 24 February 1979 is the **Mersey Trader** (GBR, 496gt/77), a product of the McTay Marine shipyard at Bromborough on the River Mersey. Sold in 1989, she was renamed **Medway Trader**.

Until the mid-1970s, maize was delivered to the Corn Products Company in Manchester by large vessels, latterly the bulk carrier **Carchester** (GBR, 9853grt/67) being dedicated to the route and, indeed, registered in Manchester. However in the 1970s it was decided to tranship the cargoes from larger vessels in Liverpool and a fleet of five purpose-built vessels was built for this task. They were operated by Bulk Cargo Handling Services Ltd, a subsidiary of the Alexandra Towing Company. The **Mersey Trader** was one of these five, and the only one to be built at the McTay yard.

(Bernard McCall)

There are two fixed road bridges of cantilever design over the Canal. The first of these is Latchford High Level Bridge in Warrington. These two bridges have always been popular with the general public and photographers as they offer excellent views of passing vessels both from the bridge itself and from the approach roads.

Passing beneath Latchford High Level Bridge on 13 July 1977 is the **Irwell Trader** (GBR, 492gt/77), another of the class noted above but built by the Yorkshire Drydock Co Ltd in Hull. She was sold to the same owner as the **Medway Trader** and was renamed **Tidal Trader**.

(Bernard McCall)

Heading west and about to pass beneath Latchford High Level Bridge on 9 September 1981 is the **Grete Theresa** (DNK, 827grt/67) built at the Krögerwerft shipyard on the bank of the Kiel Canal at Schacht-Audorf, near Rendsburg. She was sold by her Danish owners in 1990 and was renamed **Silja**, becoming **Eco** **Supporter** in 1994. Five years later, she came into British ownership when bought by J R Rix & Sons Ltd, of Hull, being renamed **Rix Condor**. She continues to trade as a bunkering tanker around the UK coast.

(John Robinson)

43

Emerging from the larger of the two lock chambers at Latchford and heading westwards is the *Pionier* (NLD, 1486gt/85), built at the Ferus Smit yard in Foxhol. In 1999, this coaster was sold to Irish operators, transferred to the Maltese flag and was renamed *Donal Paraic*. Her new life was short-lived for she foundered in December of that same year. The photograph was taken from the B5157 road which runs alongside the Canal at this point.

(John Slavin)

From the same vantage point but now looking westwards, the *Pionier* passes beneath the railway bridge at Latchford. This is one of four such railway bridges, the others being at Acton Grange, Cadishead and Irlam. They were built in 1892/3 and were initially tested by placing several heavy steam locomotives on the tracks over the bridge. Latchford bridge, carrying the London & North Western Railway's line between Warrington and Stockport, was opened for goods trains in February 1893 and for passenger trains in July of that year. Only then began excavation of the earth for the Canal at that point.

(John Slavin)

About to enter the large lock chamber at Latchford on 14 September 1995 is the *Otto* (CYP, 2037gt/70), a regular visitor to the Canal and especially to the Esso terminal at Mode Wheel (see page 70). Located 21 miles (33 kilometres) from Eastham, the locks have a rise/fall of 12' 6" (3,81 metres). The ship was built at the Krögerwerft yard in Schacht-Audorf, the second of three similar tankers built at this yard for German operator Leth & Co to whom she was handed over on 28 May 1970. All three were lengthened at the Jos L Meyer yard in Papenburg in the mid-1970s, the *Otto* being the last to be treated when fitted with a 12-metre section in September 1976. She left northern Europe in 1997 when she was sold to Greek owners who renamed her *Aegean VII* and took delivery in Hamburg in early December of that year.

(Peter Spilsbury)

An intriguing photograph that partly sums up all that is wrong about transport in the UK. During the early and mid-1990s, extensive work was done on the M6 motorway at Thelwall, with the existing single span being improved and, having been deemed inadequate, a new span built. Construction work is clearly underway on 8 May 1996 as the **Arklow Venture** (IRL, 2827gt/90) heads eastwards towards Cerestar Wharf with a cargo of maize. If a mere fraction of the money spent on the road system were to be spent on commercial waterways, many of the UK's transport problems could be eased. The River Bollin and River Mersey join the Canal just to the east of Thelwall Viaduct. The coaster is one of a series built for Arklow Shipping by the Hugo Peters shipyard at Wewelsfleth. After a decade in Arklow ownership, she was sold to German operators and renamed **Thruster** under the flag of Antigua & Barbuda.

(John Slavin)

The next crossing of the Canal is Warburton High Level Bridge, the second of the two cantilever bridges. The present bridge was built to replace a stone structure that crossed the River Mersey at this point, the river having been diverted to become part of the Canal. Heading westwards towards Latchford Locks having just passed beneath Warburton Bridge on 6 June 1979 is the **Leon Sif** (DNK, 499grt/67) built for Danish owners by the Bodewes shipyard in Hoogezand. In 1979, she was sold and renamed **Tramp Ship I**, becoming **Hafnia** in 1982 and finally **Agiantonis** under the Greek flag in 1986.

(John Slavin)

Another stern view from Warburton Bridge, but this time looking east, finds the **Ballylesson** (GBR, 1280grt/59) inward bound on 22 April 1979 almost certainly to Partington for a cargo of coal. Built by A Hall & Co, Aberdeen, she left the John Kelly fleet in 1982 and was renamed **Lino**. Further sales saw her become **Cristi** in 1987, **Samaa I** in 1992 and **G. Mother** in 1994. In June 1994, she was reported to have settled in shallow water at Porbandar in India and was presumably either demolished or allowed to rot there, but was not deleted from *Lloyd's Register* until 1998.

(John Slavin)

Beyond Warburton Bridge is a length of Canal known as the 90' Cutting. Heading westwards at this point on 1 March 1980 is the **Katerina V** (GRC, 2580grt/58). This tanker was built as **Grit** by the Goole Shipbuilding & Repairing Co Ltd for F T Everard. She spent only a decade in the Everard fleet, being sold in June 1968 to Greek owners who renamed her **Eleni**. Further sales within Greece saw her become **Katerina V** in 1973 and **Alnour** in 1985. In March 1986 she was sold to Greek breakers for demolition at Eleusis.

(John Slavin)

Situated 27 miles (43 kilometres) from Eastham is Partington Basin. Once known as Partington Coal Basin, the latter name indicates its original use. Here were located seven coal tips by means of which coal could be tipped direct from rail wagons into the bunkers of ships, and some coal was loaded as cargo even from the early days of the Canal. The tips had railway lines on two levels. The full wagon would arrive on one level, its contents tipped into the ship, then the empty wagon would roll away on the other level into sidings of which there were almost 20 miles at one time. The demise of steamships reduced the importance of the Basin but it continued to be used to load cargoes of coal. Heading westwards in July 1975 is the Stornoway-registered *Isle of Rona* (GBR, 430grt/56), ex *Ranskar*-74, *Stortemelk*-60. She was built at the Gebr. Sander yard in Delfzijl. In 1981, she was sold to other British owners and renamed *Barnstaple Trader*. She was arrested at Inverness on 24 February 1983 and eventually offered for sale in July 1984. She was towed to the Thames in December 1984 and soon resold for demolition at Queenborough.

(John Slavin)

By the late 1980s, Partington Basin was dedicated to the handling of liquefied gas, chemicals and petroleum products many of these being generated by Shell's huge chemical complex at nearby Carrington. At this time only four berths were in use, numbers 2, 4 and 6 on the south side of the Basin and number 1 on the north side. At the latter berth on 26 March 1994 is the **Jersbek** (LIB, 2690gt/82), ex **Cape Island**-87, built at the Büsumer Werft shipyard. This view should be compared to that on the previous page, taken from a similar vantage point albeit with a telephoto lens for the **Jersbek**.

(John Slavin)

The coal tips at Partington gradually disappeared in the 1970s as the Lancashire coalfield dwindled in size and soon the only tip which remained was used mainly to load soda ash, some of which was exported to South Africa. Judging by the covered railway wagons waiting on the tip, the **Musketier II** (ANT, 1353grt/67) was waiting to load soda ash when photographed on 1 February 1980. She was built at the "De Vooruitgang" yard in Alphen a/d Rijn as **Browersgracht** , becoming **Musketier II** in 1977. Following sale in 1984, she was renamed **Shah Sahib** and then **Kulsawn** in 1988.

(John Slavin)

52

On 15 September 1991, two sisterships arrived from Zaandam to discharge silos for one of the nearby chemical plants, the **Transportör** (ATG, 2875gt/90) and **Ruth** (DEU, 2873gt/91). They were built at the J G Hitzler shipyard in Lauenburg and completed at the Peterswerft yard in Rendsburg although *Lloyd's Register* notes that the **Transportör** was built entirely at the Hitzler yard. Both vessels sailed later in the day but to very different destinations. The **Transportör** sailed across the Atlantic to Parrsboro in Nova Scotia whilst **Ruth** sailed to Dunball Wharf in Somerset. The latter vessel continues to trade under her original name but in July 2004 the **Transportör** arrived in Szczecin to be converted into a cement carrier and now trades as **Cemsky**.

(John Slavin)

On 31 August 2003, evidently a still day, the **Stolt Cormorant** (CYM, 3818gt/99) lies at Partington's No. 2 berth. In the background is Cadishead railway viaduct, no longer used by trains and with tracks lifted. The double-hulled tanker was built at the Affini shipyard in La Spezia. Stolt tankers have become the most frequent visitors to Partington in recent years and the cargoes handled are mainly styrene, propylene oxide and monopropylene glycol which are feedstock for the Shell's Carrington installation. Part of this is scheduled for closure and this will reduce the number of vessels using the Canal.

(Bernard McCall)

Half a mile (800 metres) from Partington on the northern bank of the Canal is Irlam Wharf. This was established to serve the local steel works and was used mainly for the import of iron and manganese ore. The Partington Steel and Iron Company opened the first steel works on the site in 1910. Twenty years later, various mergers resulted in the formation of the Lancashire Steel Corporation and huge quantities were produced until the nationalisation of the steel industry in the 1960s. Then steel production started to decline and it had ceased entirely by 1979. The wharf was no longer used but surprisingly was reactivated in the mid-1990s. This revival seems to have produced only two cargoes. However 2004 saw the establishment of a container service linking the Canal to Southampton and Greenock. At the time of writing in early 2006, there were two vessels on the route one of these being the **Philipp** (ATG, 2567gt/78). Built at the J J Sietas yard on the outskirts of Hamburg, she is an example of that yard's Type 96 standard design, one of several such designs developed to serve the rapidly-growing container feeder trades in the 1970s. Launched as **Karat**, she was immediately renamed **Magnolia** but reverted to **Karat** before the end of 1978. Subsequent name changes have been **Ile de France** (1982), **Rhein Lagan** (1993), **Karat** (1994), **Philipp** (1994), **SCL Clipper** (1997) and **Philipp** (1998).

(Rosalind Thomas)

Approaching Irlam Locks on 19 July 1997 is the **Arklow Fortune** (IRL, 2373gt/92). There are signs of the dark green hull she had when under her original name of **MB Humber**. Built at the Ferus Smit shipyard in Foxhol, she joined the Arklow Shipping fleet in 1997. She and her three sisterships were regular visitors to Cerestar Wharf (see page 68) with maize from French Bay ports such as Bayonne. She was sold in February 2005 to Norwegian owners who renamed her **Bimi** under the Bahamas flag although she was chartered back to Arklow Shipping for a short time. Between Irlam Wharf and Irlam Locks where there are five sluices, the River Mersey flows into the Canal. The railway bridge at Irlam takes the former Cheshire Lines Committee line linking Manchester and Liverpool over the Canal.

(John Slavin)

The **Shevrell** (IRL, 1393gt/81) is making fast in Irlam Locks during a westbound passage along the Canal in August 1988 having discharged maize at Cerestar Wharf. Built at the Niestern Sander yard in Delfzijl, she was lengthened by 8 metres in 1991. In January 1998, she was sold to Norwegian owners and renamed **Garibaldi**, moving on in 2004 to Lebanese owners by whom she was renamed **Ghofran**. There is presently so little traffic on the upper section of the Canal that Irlam and the two further locks to be passed on passage to Manchester are staffed by a single crew who drive from one site to another as required. However when all sets of locks were fully manned, there was fierce rivalry in the annual contest to have the best maintained gardens and buildings.

(John Slavin)

Leaving Irlam Locks and heading eastwards past the crossing point of a former foot ferry is the **Albert V** (NLD, 494gt/65). She has sailed almost 8 miles (12 kilometres) from Latchford Locks and she will have been raised by 16' (4,88 metres) at Irlam. She was operated by International Shipbrokers whose small fleet was always maintained in immaculate condition. Built by "De Vooruitgang" v/h D Boot shipyard at Alphen a/d Rijn as **Breewijd**, she became **Albert V** in 1974. After a decade as such, she was bought by Mediterranean operators and renamed **Ikaros**. A further decade of service followed before she was renamed **Shamsddin III** and was converted to a livestock carrier. She remains listed as such in the 2005/6 edition of *Lloyd's Register*. The photograph was taken in June 1970.

(Ken Lowe)

Making her only appearance on the Canal, the former east coast collier *Cliff Quay* (GBR, 3345grt/50) is seen between Irlam and Barton on 16 November 1983. This was her final voyage of any kind because she had been sold for demolition at Manchester. She was built by Wm Pickersgill & Sons at Southwick, Sunderland, and had spent her entire career carrying coal from ports in eastern Scotland and north-east England to power stations in the south and south-east. There were proposals to preserve her or one of her sisterships but these were never likely to come to fruition.

(John Slavin)

On the south side of the Canal near Barton Locks is Davyhulme harbour built to accommodate the effluent tankers which loaded effluent from the North West Water Authority and delivered it to Liverpool Bay for disposal at sea. This method of effluent disposal ended in the late 1990s by which time the effluent had ceased to be loaded at Davyhulme but rather in Liverpool. However the loading arms are still visible in this view of the *Ardent* (GBR, 700gt/83) making her way up the Canal in pouring rain on 13 August 2004 with a piece of heavy electrical equipment loaded at Leith. The *Ardent* is another product of the Yorkshire Drydock Co Ltd and represents a design that came to be known as the "Yorkshire Coaster".

(Bernard McCall)

We have already noted that an ideal way to obtain photographs of vessels on the Canal is from one of the cruises operated by Mersey Ferries. Sometimes, the passenger has the good fortune to find his/her ferry sharing a lock with another vessel and this happened on 26 July 2001 when the *Gina D* (GBR, 507gt/75) accompanied the ferry along the Canal and was photographed as she emerged from Barton Locks. The design of this ship should be compared to that of the *Ardent* on the previous page for it was on the *Gina D* and her sisterships that the "Yorkshire Coaster" design was closely based. Another product of the Yorkshire Drydock Co Ltd, the *Gina D* was built as *Seaborne Trader* and traded as such until 1987 when imports to Cerestar began to come directly from France rather than being transhipped at Liverpool. Her new owners renamed her *Island Swift*

and traded her in the south-east of England and more general coasting. In 1990, she was sold again, renamed *Yeoman Rose* and began to operate in a very different transhipment trade for she now loaded cargoes of stone brought from the huge Foster Yeoman quarry at Glensanda to the Isle of Grain. From there she delivered the stone to smaller ports in the south-east, usually Whitstable. She also loaded stone at Calais for Whitstable or Ridham Dock. Displaced from this trade in 1997, she was chartered in the summer of that year to work as a floating radio station off the Essex coast as part of the Radio London 30th anniversary celebrations. She then returned to lay up until purchased by KD Marine who renamed her *Gina D*, and she returned to work on the Canal in May 1999.

(Dominic McCall)

The rise in Barton Locks is 15 feet (4,57 metres). In the large lock is the **Authority** (GBR, 500grt/67) which has just left Barton Oil Berth on a sunny day in late 1969. Once again we can note the enthusiasm with which the staff maintained the gardens. Other features are the accumulator tower which provides the water pressure to work the hydraulic gate machinery (a gauge on the gateman's cabin shows the available pressure); a railway wagon in the siding; and the height gauge tower whose wire seems to be missing, suggesting that a ship had had a recent altercation with it. The **Authority** was built at the Nieuwe Noord-Nederlandse shipyard in Groningen and was slightly smaller than three other tankers later built at this yard for the Everard company. Sold to Greek owners in 1985, she was renamed **Sosco I**, becoming **Georgios S** in 1987, **Georgios** in 1989, and **Aegean I** in 1993. One of her Greek owners is reported to have built a garage on deck to accommodate road tankers which distributed fuel on smaller Greek islands. She currently works as a bunkering tanker in the Piraeus area.

(Ken Lowe)

On page 46, we noted the bridge which carried the M6 motorway over the Canal at Thelwall near Warrington. Just east of Barton Locks, the M60 crosses the Canal on a bridge built in the early 1960s for what was then the Stretford - Eccles bypass. During construction, the central span of this bridge fell into the Canal as it was being slotted into place. Passing beneath the bridge in March 1984 is the

Hopper No. 26 (GBR, 941gt/54) built by W Simons & Co Ltd at Renfrew. She and sister vessel **Hopper No. 25** were hopper barges and worked on the Clyde for the Clyde Port Authority. Both were towed along the Canal for demolition at Manchester.

(John Slavin)

Coaster movements on the upper reaches of the Canal are now dominated by vessels of the Arklow Shipping fleet which deliver maize to Cerestar Wharf as we see on page 68. The Arklow company's acquisition of Dutch shipowners Hanno in 1999 occasionally resulted in vessels other than the green-hulled Arklow coasters calling at Cerestar Wharf. On 6 September 2000, the **Marjolein** (NLD, 2715gt/94), built at the Bijholt shipyard in Foxhol and formerly in the Hanno fleet, heads down the Canal having delivered maize from Bordeaux to Cerestar. She has just passed through Barton road bridge and, immediately before that, Barton aqueduct which carries the Bridgewater Canal over the Manchester Ship Canal and is one of the most interesting engineering structures along the Canal.

(Steve Ingram)

On the south bank of the Canal just east of the Barton Aqueduct was Barton Oil Berth. Once again, Shell was the main user of this berth with three C-class tankers specially built to serve the berth bringing lubricating oil from the Caribbean from the mid-1950s until the late 1970s. Although Esso tankers were never usual visitors, on 13 July 1991 the **Esso Penzance** (GBR, 2144gt/71) leaves the Barton berth. One of three almost identical sisterships built by Appledore Shipbuilders, each originally had a dedicated distribution role and the **Esso Penzance** was intended to handle kerosene, motor spirit and some lubricating oils, the latter probably explaining her call at Barton. Renamed **Petro Penzance** in 1994 when oil companies were anxious about making an obvious association with their ships following some high profile spillages, she entered the F T Everard fleet in 1995 and was renamed **Assurity**. After only two years trading as such, she was sold to Greek owners by whom she was renamed **Medoil II**.

(Roy Cressey)

A footpath along the southern bank of the Canal used to offer excellent views of Irwell Park Wharf on the northern bank. The wharf's sole use now is the export of scrap but in the past it has been used for the import of ores, sulphur and bulk cargoes. Observed there in the early 1970s was the **Spartan Spirit** (LBR, 919grt/58), built by de Groot & van Vliet at Slikkerveer. The coaster was launched as **Con Amore** but seems to have entered service as **Monte Cinto**. In 1963 she was sold and renamed **Leptis**, then becoming **Gaelic** in 1969 and **Spartan Spirit** in 1970. She traded as such until 1974 when she was sold again, this time becoming **Skystewart** and working in the clay trade to the Mediterranean. In 1982, she was sold on to Lebanese buyers and renamed **Marsi III**. Her later history remains obscure.

(John Slavin)

As hinted at on the previous page, the path which could once be used to take photographs of ships is no longer available. So we offer another view from years gone by, with the **Marie-Louise** (FRA, 1542grt/58) at the wharf on 28 November 1976. Built by Abeking & Rasmussen at Lemwerder, this vessel was initially named **Inga Bastian** and was lengthened in 1959. She came into French ownership in 1974 and remained with these owners until 1978 when she was sold and renamed **Crusader**. In 1984, she was sold again and renamed **Eolos**, eventually disappearing from *Lloyd's Register* in 2001. There has never been a particularly large French coaster fleet so the inclusion of this vessel is of significance.

(John Slavin)

Trafford Park was the ancestral home of the de Trafford family and occupied a site between the Bridgewater Canal and River Irwell. In 1896, the Park was sold to a speculator who wished to establish an industrial estate there. This became the first purpose-built industrial estate in the world. The twin attractions of direct deep-water access and a rail system connected both to the national main lines and to the Canal's own extensive private rail network resulted in rapid growth. One of the first companies to open in Trafford Park was Nicholls Nagle which eventually became Corn Products Company Ltd and supplied a wide range of refined corn products to a range of customers. Now known as Cerestar UK and a part of the Cargill group, the company processes more than 1000 tonnes of maize daily to extract starch, protein oils and fibre which is used in the paper and pharmaceutical industries in addition to food. Discharging maize on 26 July 2001 is the **Arklow Faith** (IRL, 2373gt/92), ex **MB Thames**-97, built at the Ferus Smit yard in Foxhol and a sistership of the **Arklow Fortune** noted on page 56. In mid-2005, she followed the latter to Norwegian ownership and was renamed **Romi**.

(Bernard McCall)

The Cerestar mill and glucose refinery is one of the largest in Europe and enjoys constant development. Not only is the Ship Canal ideal for importing raw materials but it can also be used for the delivery of heavy equipment. On 16 June 1997, the *Silvia* (DEU, 1587gt/84) discharges a new silo which had been brought from Buckie in north-east Scotland. Built at the Husumer shipyard, she was acquired by Scotline in 1998 and was renamed *Scot Pioneer* at the end of January 1998 since when she has worked in the timber trades for that company.

(John Slavin)

Everard tankers have always been regular visitors to the Canal and here we see the **Annuity** (GBR, 1599grt/61) swinging off Mode Wheel oil berth. It is likely that she was not berthing here, though, because she usually carried lubricating oils from Rotterdam to Barton oil berth and may simply have been swinging to go back down the Canal to Barton. Like other Everard tankers featured in this book, she was sold to Greek owners and has continued to give excellent service in the Mediterranean. Her first sale was in 1983 and she became **Thita Triena**, and subsequent sales within Greece saw her renamed **Blue Eyes** in 1986, **Jet VI** in 1987 and **Promitheus** in 1988.

(John Slavin)

The final locks on our journey towards Manchester are Mode Wheel Locks which have a rise of 13' (3,96 metres). It must not be forgotten that efforts had been made to enable boats to reach Manchester prior to the Canal's construction with the Mersey & Irwell Navigation Company building locks and weirs to assist navigation. It is assumed that the name Mode Wheel came from a wheel (Maud's Wheel) which was driven by the fall of water over a weir at this location, the wheel powering a long-established corn mill. Emerging from the lock on 17 October 2005 and about to approach the berth where she will discharge grain for Rank Hovis is the **Anna D** (GBR, 633gt/76). Built by for F T Everard by the J W Cook shipyard at Wivenhoe, she traded as **Celebrity** for most of her life even when sold out of the Everard fleet. In 2004, she was bought by Runcorn-based K D Marine for trade on the Ship Canal.

(Rosalind Thomas)

From the outset, the Manchester Ship Canal Company decided that ship repair facilities would be required in Manchester and a site was set aside for this. Initially a small graving dock was built and two more were later added along with a pontoon. With traffic on the Canal in decline, the drydocks closed in 1979 only to reopen about four years later when the main work was ship demolition. Closure and reopening has continued over the last two decades. Noted alongside the drydocks in autumn 1986 is the *Glenhaven* (IOM, 560grt/57), launched as *Jan T* by builders IJsselwerf at Rotterdam but entering service as *Cambrian Coast*. Sold in 1971, she was renamed *Lorraine D* and traded as such for a decade before becoming *Zircon* in 1981 and finally *Glenhaven* in 1982. After being laid up in Birkenhead since 1981, she moved to Manchester for drydocking in preparation for a return to trade. In fact, she never traded again, but returned to lay up in Birkenhead. Sold by the Admiralty Marshal, she was towed away from Birkenhead on 22 June 1988, bound for scrapping in Milford Haven.

(John Slavin)

We are now in the terminal docks and in the distance of this view can be seen Mode Wheel Locks. With rain clearly approaching from the west, a rare shaft of sunlight highlights the **Loke** (DNK, 300grt/70) as she swings off No. 9 Dock on 22 March 1979. At this date, container ships still used the port although a decision had been made to transfer the Manchester Liners' transatlantic service to Liverpool where larger vessels could be accommodated. Some of the company's own distinctive containers are stored on the quayside in this view. The coaster was built at the Nordsøvĺrftet yard in Ringkøbing. On 5 October 1973, she sank after a collision in the River Weser, but she was raised and towed to Århus for repair, returning to service at the end of the year. Sold in 1982, she was renamed **Ocean Trader**, becoming **Hong Soon** in 1988 and **Lian Lestari 5** in 2000. As such, she is registered in Jakarta and continues to trade in Indonesia.

(John Slavin)

It is difficult to imagine that this dock would once have been filled with ocean-going cargo ships and that transit sheds lined the quayside at the right hand side of the photograph whilst container vessels would use the berth on the left where the gantry cranes still stood at the time of this view, 28 June 1990. The **Danica White** (DNK, 997gt/85), built by Sakskøbing Maskinfabrik og Skibsværft, pulls away from No. 1 Berth in No. 9 Dock having discharged a cargo of timber from Leixoes.

(John Slavin)

Wagenborg's **Waalborg** (NLD, 513grt/56) has arrived in No. 9 Dock on a Sunday in April 1971. The next morning she will discharge her grain cargo by means of the floating pneumatic elevator into one of the conveyor belts in subways beneath the quays and delivered to the huge No. 2 grain silo at the end of the dock. No. 9 Dock was built after the other docks. It was in 1901 that the Manchester Ship Canal Company purchased the site of Manchester racecourse and began construction of the new dock. When completed four years later, it was twice as long as the previous largest dock, No. 8. The **Waalborg** was sold to Greek owners in 1974 and was renamed **Paleoupolis**, later becoming **Caicos Express** in 1981. She sank on 12 November 1985.

(Ken Lowe)

Photographed at No. 8 Pier on 27 June 1980 is the **Trostan** (GBR, 486gt/64), a coaster with a troubled late career and subsequent demise. Built by Goole Shipbuilding & Repairing Co Ltd, she began life as **Northgate** and traded as a container vessel on the Irish Sea. In 1979, she was sold, renamed **Trostan**, and entered the general cargo trades. Sold again two years later, she was renamed **Pekari**, later becoming **Elmham** in 1989 and **Tia** in 1992. It was during her time under this name that her troubles began. Arriving with steering problems at Castletownbere in November 1996 following an Atlantic crossing, it was claimed that drugs were on board but extensive searches proved to be in vain. She remained there until June 2000 when she sailed to Barry. Transferred to the Panamanian flag and renamed **Beatrice II**, she was reported to be destined for use in the Scottish timber trade but after arrival at Campbeltown on 17 August 2000, she was laid up with mechanical problems. In July 2001, she was sold again and was towed to Portsmouth where she was eventually demolished in 2002.

(John Slavin)

The wharf opposite No. 6 to No. 9 Docks was Trafford Wharf and this too was busy with shipping activity, mainly cargoes of grain. Discharging at the large British Oil & Cake Mills premises on 30 April 1976 is the **Skjevik** (NOR, 499grt/69). This coaster had only just been renamed, having traded as **Cathrine Lonborg** until earlier in the year and **Merc Astra** until 1973. She was a product of the Oberwinter shipyard in Remagen. Lengthened in 1977, she had a whole string of names following her sale in 1983 which saw her become **Hammervik**. These names were **Isi Team** (1984), **Sea Team** (1989), **Haj Mohammed** (1990), **H. J. M. 1** (1991), **Sea Pride** and **Gaye** (1999). Her end came on 18 July 2000 when she sank while on passage from Constanta to Damietta with parts for a sugar refinery.

(John Slavin)

It is pleasing to note that one of the original five vessels built to carry grain from Liverpool to Manchester (see page 42) continues in this work. We have already seen the *Gina D* but we now note her as she prepares to leave her discharge berth in Manchester on 26 July 2001 at the start of a voyage to Liverpool. An unusually busy scene is completed by several hopper barges moored outside the drydocks and just visible to the left in a drydock is the *Arneb* (DEU, 3640gt/86), ex *Alster Rapid*-95, the solitary Type 136 ship from the J J Sietas yard. She had arrived two days previously to be converted to a nuclear fuel carrier and emerged under the name *Atlantic Osprey*.

(Dominic McCall)

A panoramic view of part of the dock area as the *Hoo Willow* (GBR, 671gt/84) discharges a piece of heavy equipment on 5 July 2003. She lies at the berth that would have been used by Manchester Liners container ships and was seen from a different viewpoint on pages 73 and 74. In the upper part of the photograph, the western end of Trafford Wharf has been given over to the storage of lorries, a reflection of the changed emphasis in transport.

(John Slavin)

At the planning stage, it had been intended to build the terminal docks on the Manchester and Stretford side of the Canal but in 1888 it was decided to build the main docks on the Salford side where there was more room for expansion. Eventually, there were four small upstream docks in Manchester, known as Pomona Docks. These were intended for coastal vessels and perishable goods. Latterly they were used for heavy lifts. The docks were numbered 1 to 4; No. 5 dock was never built but if it had been, it would have been a long wharf rather than single dock.

The heavy-lift vessels using these docks displayed various profiles. One of the more unusual types, and certainly winning no awards for beauty, was the **Mariaeck** (DEU, 687grt/69), photographed on 29 June 1977. Built at the T Duijvendijk shipyard in Lekkerkerk, she was sold in 1981 and renamed **Mari-Lift**, later becoming **Jellyn** in 1985, **Spring** in 1987 and **Agia Kyriaki** in 1995. She grounded in the Aegean whilst on passage to Piraeus on 1 December 1998. After being refloated on 14 December, she was towed to Kos. The 2001/2 edition of *Lloyd's Register* suggested that her entry should be deleted in view of her doubtful continued existence, but another source suggests that she remains in service. Visible in the background is the bow of J & A Gardner's **Saint Bedan** (GBR, 1251grt/72).

(John Slavin)

Opposite Pomona Docks, and not too far from where the proposed No. 5 Dock would have been, was Colgate's Wharf. The usual cargo to be discharged here was silica sand, usually loaded in Norway and delivered by coasters in the J & A Gardner fleet. In July 1966, Gardner's **Saint Blane** (GBR, 680grt/55) was discharging her cargo. Built at the Port Glasgow shipyard of James Lamont & Co Ltd, she was launched on 23 June 1955 and left the Gardner fleet in 1971 when she was renamed **Gulf Planet**. Five years later, she was sold again and renamed **Zuhair** but traded for only two more years before being sold to Egyptian shipbreakers and on 12 January 1979 she arrived at Suez for demolition.

The silica sand discharged at this wharf would be used mainly in "Ajax" scouring powder. Such pure sand has continued to be imported to the Manchester Ship Canal but has been loaded at Lochaline in Scotland, discharged at Runcorn and has been destined for use in the glass industry.

(Ken Lowe)

The photographer would have been standing on Trafford Wharf to take this photograph of the **Derwent Fisher** (GBR, 999grt/80) as she sailed through the dock system in April 1975 when some demolition of warehouses was already underway as can be seen at the far right of the photograph. Built at the Nieuwe Noord-Nederlandse shipyard in Groningen for James Fisher, she had a succession of names (some displaying poor knowledge of English!) after leaving the Fisher fleet in 1979, becoming **Parham** and then **Sofia** in 1984, **Saint Anthonys** in 1989, **Golduen Bird** in 1990, **Maria** and then **Swene** in 1991 and **Baris B** in 1996. She was still trading as such in mid-2002 but her fate since then is unknown.

(John Slavin)

The view from Trafford Wharf in 2006 is astonishingly different. Although commercial vessels no longer sail to this part of the dock system, dredging is necessary to remove silt which comes from the rivers flowing into the docks. The Manchester Ship Canal Company used to have its own fleet of dredgers but as the requirements changed with declining traffic in the 1980s, a joint study was undertaken by the Company and Westminster Dredging, the outcome of which was the disposal of the Company's own fleet and a long-term contract for maintenance dredging being awarded to Westminster Dredging. The dredger used is the **W. D. Severn** (GBR, 1337gt/74), built at the Verolme yard in Heusden. She is seen at work on 5 March 2006.

(Bernard McCall)